Need to Know
HIV and AIDS

Sean Connolly

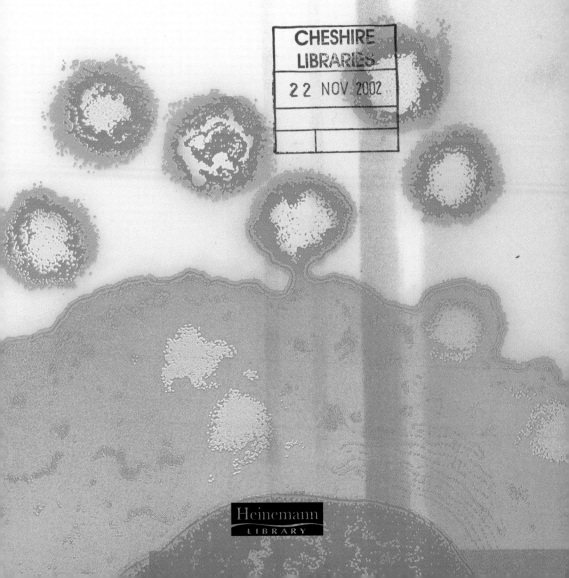

Heinemann
LIBRARY

www.heinemann.co.uk
visit our website to find out more information about **Heinemann Library** books.

To order:
☎ Phone 44 (0) 1865 888066
🖹 Send a fax to 44 (0) 1865 314091
💻 Visit the Heinemann Bookshop at www.heinemann.co.uk to browse our catalogue and order online.

First published in Great Britain by Heinemann Library, Halley Court, Jordan Hill, Oxford OX2 8EJ,
a division of Reed Educational and Professional Publishing Ltd.
Heinemann is a registered trademark of Reed Educational & Professional Publishing Limited.

Oxford Melbourne Auckland Johannesburg Blantyre Gaborone Ibadan Portsmouth NH (USA) Chicago

Designed by M2 Graphic Design
Originated by Ambassador Litho Ltd
Printed in China by South China Printers

ISBN 0431 097968

06 05 04 03 02
10 9 8 7 6 5 4 3 2 1

British Library Cataloguing in Publication Data
Connolly, Sean,
HIV and AIDS. – (Need to Know)
1. HIV (Viruses) – Juvenile literature
2. AIDS (Disease) – Juvenile literature
I. Title
362.1'9'69792

Acknowledgements
The publishers would like to thank the following for permission to reproduce photographs: Corbis pp10, 11,
12, 25, 32, 35, 36, 41, 44, 45, 46, Getty Images p31, Minnesota AIDS Project p42, Panos Pictures pp13,
22, Photofusion pp27, 39, 43, 50, 51, Popperfoto pp17, 21, 23, 38, Rex Features p29, Robert Harding
Picture Library pp5, 18, 19, 49, Science Photo Library pp6, 9, 15, 24, 33, 47, The Stock Market p7.

Cover photographs reproduced with permission of Science Photo Library, Photodisc and
Telegraph Colour Library.

Every effort has been made to contact copyright holders of any material reproduced in this book.
Any omissions will be rectified in subsequent printings if notice is given to the publisher.

Contents

Any words appearing in the text in bold, **like this**, are explained in the Glossary.

HIV and AIDS

One of the most alarming medical problems ever faced is now striking fear into most parts of the world. This deadly enemy is HIV, an infection that leads to the wasting condition known as AIDS. It has grown from being an unknown condition to being a 'public enemy' in a very short period of time.

Deadly arrival

Since it was first identified about twenty years ago, the HIV virus has been linked to a series of medical problems. These eventually weaken the body and leave it defenceless against infection. With the body's natural defences destroyed, infections that would normally be fought off – including **pneumonia**, **tuberculosis** and even flu – can become killers. Sometimes people don't even notice the initial infection – caused by the HIV virus – that leads to this weakened state.

Easily passed on, HIV can sweep across entire regions, infecting large proportions of the population. In some of the worst-affected areas, nearly two thirds of the new infections occur among people aged 16–25. Many of these young people will soon lose the ability to work – and they might well die – within a decade. These are not 'scare stories'. Parts of Africa are already experiencing the widespread infection that scientists had predicted less than a decade ago. This problem will extend far beyond health: with no one well enough – or even alive – to perform essential jobs, entire countries could face the virtual disintegration of their economies.

The response

The news is not, or perhaps need not be, all bad. In the two decades of medical research into HIV and AIDS, scientists have isolated the virus that causes the infection and have studied it closely. Based on their findings, public health officials and AIDS charities have been able to send out clear signals about how the infection is passed on. More importantly they can show how it can be prevented from being **transmitted**. The enemy in their fight is not just the deadly combination of HIV and AIDS. It is the stubbornness of many people who will not understand the simple message: ignorance is death.

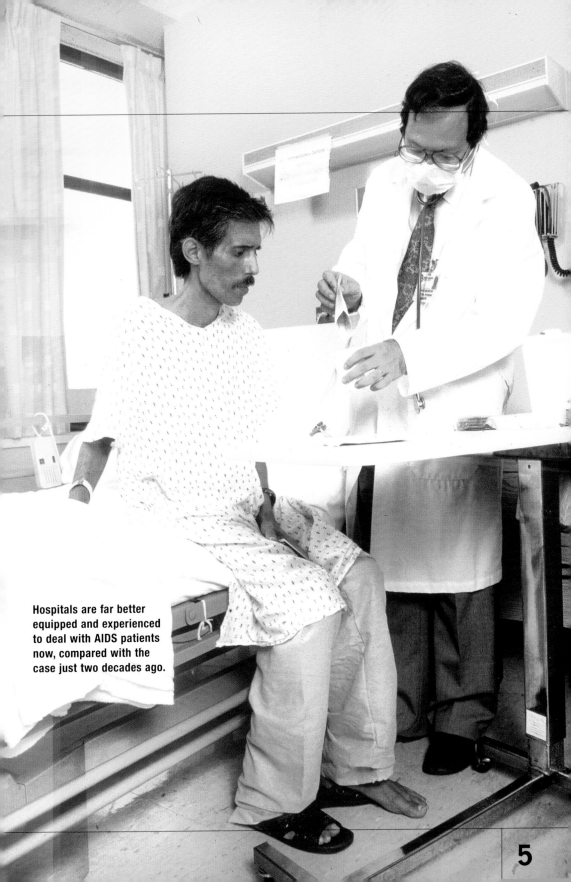

Hospitals are far better equipped and experienced to deal with AIDS patients now, compared with the case just two decades ago.

What are HIV and AIDS?

Possibly the two most alarming medical abbreviations – both for individuals and for society at large – are HIV and AIDS. The first, HIV, stands for Human Immunodeficiency Virus. It leads to the disease AIDS, or Acquired Immune Deficiency **Syndrome**. Although the two abbreviations usually appear together, it is important to understand that HIV is a virus, while AIDS is a syndrome.

Viruses are specific organisms that can be located within the body, even if they cannot be destroyed. A syndrome, on the other hand, describes a medical condition that has many **symptoms**.

In practical terms, this difference is very important. Doctors can perform a specific test to see whether the HIV virus is present in the blood. To **diagnose** AIDS (a syndrome) they must detect a combination of symptoms, not one single kind of germ. These symptoms are the result of infections that develop because of the body's weakened ability to fight them off. Although there are many different types of such infection, their ability to take advantage of the weakened **immune system** gives them the medical name **'opportunistic infection'**.

Contracting the virus

The HIV virus is most commonly spread by sexual contact with an infected person. It is present in the sexual **secretions** of infected men and women and can gain access to the bloodstream of an uninfected person by way of small cuts or **abrasions** that may occur as a consequence of sexual intercourse. As membranes are so thin in the sexual organs, infection can also occur where there are no abrasions. HIV is also spread by any sharing of needles or syringes that leads to direct exposure to the blood of an infected individual. This method of exposure occurs most commonly among people injecting **intravenous** (IV) drugs. HIV can also be transmitted from an infected mother to her baby, either before or during

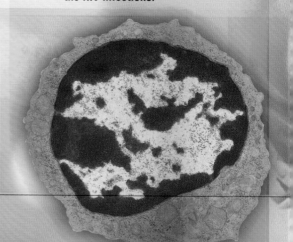

Many new tests help diagnose and monitor the HIV infections.

childbirth, or through breastfeeding. Although only about 20 to 30 per cent of babies born to HIV-infected mothers actually become infected, this mode of transmission accounts for 90 per cent of all cases of AIDS in children.

Some methods of HIV transmission have been virtually wiped out, and other suspected methods have now been shown to be harmless. When the HIV virus was first identified in the 1980s, there was concern that HIV could be spread through blood **transfusions**. By the mid-1980s, most countries had set up screening systems to ensure that such blood is safe. In the USA now, for example, it is estimated that undetected HIV is present in fewer than 1 in 450,000 to 600,000 units of blood.

Other instances, once thought to be risky, have now been shown to be safe. Studies have shown no evidence that HIV can be transmitted by insects such as mosquitoes. Similarly, it is not possible to pick up the virus by shaking hands with an infected person, or by sharing cutlery.

The major type of HIV in the USA, Europe, and central Africa is known as HIV-1. In western Africa, AIDS is also caused by HIV-2, a strain of HIV closely related to HIV-1. Other distantly related strains of HIV-1 have been identified in various areas of the world.

Intravenous drug use is another high-risk activity – the infection is passed on when people share needles.

How the body is affected

The HIV virus attacks the body's **immune system**. It weakens the body until **opportunistic infections** can set in and the patient develops fully blown AIDS. Unlike fully developed AIDS, HIV is often completely **symptom**-free. That is why it is important that people be tested for HIV if they think they might be at risk, because otherwise they would not know whether or not they had it. Sometimes symptoms occur within a few weeks after infection; these are often flu-like, such as fatigue, fever, swollen **lymph glands**, diarrhoea and night sweats.

Symptoms of AIDS are more varied, since AIDS often involves several different infections. Some common symptoms are the infections themselves (including a cancer called **Kaposi's sarcoma**, other unusual cancers, **pneumonia** and **tuberculosis**), significant weight loss, memory and eyesight problems, or symptoms of a yeast infection such as white spots in the mouth or a vaginal discharge. Of course, most of these symptoms can usually relate to conditions that are far less serious than HIV and AIDS.

Doctors and health officials urge HIV-positive people, in other words those who have tested positive for the presence of the virus, to have regular tests to monitor the progress of the disease. Some medical treatments, notably **antiviral** drugs, can slow the progress of the virus. Medical personnel monitor this progress by checking many symptoms, especially the presence of 'T4 cells' (often called simply **T-cells**). T-cells are part of the immune system. A normal T-cell count is between 500 and 1000 cells per cubic metre of blood. Medications that slow the progress of the HIV virus help keep the T-cell count relatively high; a low count is often a signal that the HIV infection has progressed to AIDS.

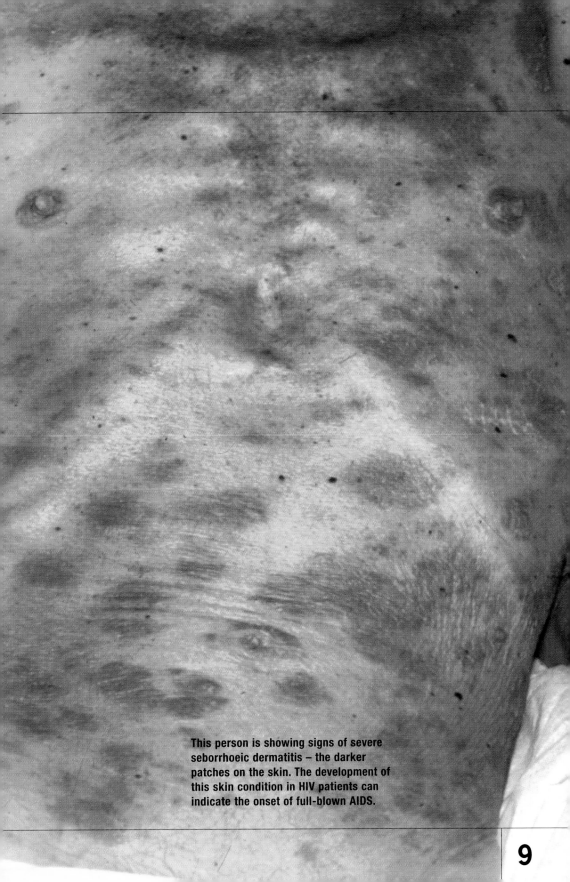

This person is showing signs of severe seborrhoeic dermatitis – the darker patches on the skin. The development of this skin condition in HIV patients can indicate the onset of full-blown AIDS.

A worldwide problem

The AIDS **epidemic** has touched every inhabited continent. At the beginning of 2001, nearly 37 million people around the world carried the HIV virus – 4 per cent of these were younger than 16. That number had doubled in only five years. Certain regions, particularly southern Africa and South-East Asia, have very high concentrations of the infection. For example, in early 2001 there were eight southern African countries in which more than fifteen per cent of the adult population carried the HIV infection. The saddest news is that every day, more than 15,000 people worldwide (nearly half of them women) are infected with HIV – that is 1 person every 11 seconds. The vast majority of these people will never have access to the new drug therapies before they die.

Effects of the increase

Medical professionals use the term 'generalized' to describe a national occurrence of HIV that is still relatively small – below one per cent. That means that the HIV virus is present in distinct groups of people – for example, male homosexuals or **intravenous** drug users – or it occurs in certain urban areas but much less widely in the countryside. The nature of HIV infection and **transmission**, however, is constantly changing and the figure of one per cent national infection can easily jump into the next category – known as 'local epidemic'. India and many East European countries, for example, seem poised to enter this higher-risk category.

This UNICEF shelter in Thailand provides a refuge for former prostitutes, now suffering from AIDS.

The effects of HIV and AIDS infection are far-reaching. In badly affected countries, such as Botswana, the entire national economy suffers. In high-prevalence areas, more than 60 per cent of new infections occur among people aged 16 to 25. Many of these people will be too ill to work, or even dead, within a decade. There will be acute shortages of labour in essential jobs and even now many schools are forced to close because the teachers are dying.

USA figures

Some of the first cases of AIDS were reported in the USA. In the last twenty years the US figures about the progress of HIV and AIDS have been among the most detailed of any country. At the beginning of 2001, over 774,450 people had been reported with AIDS in the USA; 448,060 of these had died. The number of people living with AIDS – again at the beginning of 2001 – was the highest ever reported at 322,865.

YOU'VE GOT BLOOD ON YOUR HANDS,

NYC AIDS CARE DOESN'T EXIST.

MAROON
FOR CONSPIRACY TO CREATE DEF RHYMES AND RHYTHMS, RAP WITH THE INTENT TO PLEASE, AND PUTTING UP POSTERS IN THE SUBWAY. YOUR REWARD IS THE FUNKY RECORD.

Posters and other forms of publicity keep the HIV and AIDS issue prominent in New York City.

Origins of the epidemic

Genuine cases of HIV and AIDS infection might be found by examining centuries-old medical records. However, the public awareness dates back only about two decades and concerns research carried out in California. In 1980–81 Dr Michael Gottleib of Los Angeles recognized a pattern among five young and previously healthy male patients who had contracted a rare form of **pneumonia**. Two of them had died and the other three were seriously ill. The disease usually affected people whose **immune systems** were suppressed because of drugs or disease. However, it was hard to draw any conclusions beyond the similarities in age and lifestyle.

These findings were published in a specialist medical journal *(Morbidity and Mortality Weekly Report)*, leading other physicians to announce similar findings. At about the same time, the Centers for Disease Control and Prevention (CDC), the leading USA organization monitoring such **epidemics**, noticed an alarming rate of a rare cancer called **Kaposi's sarcoma** in otherwise healthy homosexual men. Scientists now know that Kaposi's sarcoma is just one of the many conditions that can develop at the onset of AIDS – no matter how the initial HIV infection was acquired. In 1981 however, it was branded with the term 'gay cancer'. Further research led to it being linked to a wider condition, called GRID ('gay-related immune deficiency'). The new term showed that doctors saw that the real problem lay in the immune system. By this time, late 1981, there was a growing sense of urgency: 422 cases had been **diagnosed** in the USA alone and 159 people had died.

The AIDS condition was first observed among San Francisco's prominent gay population.

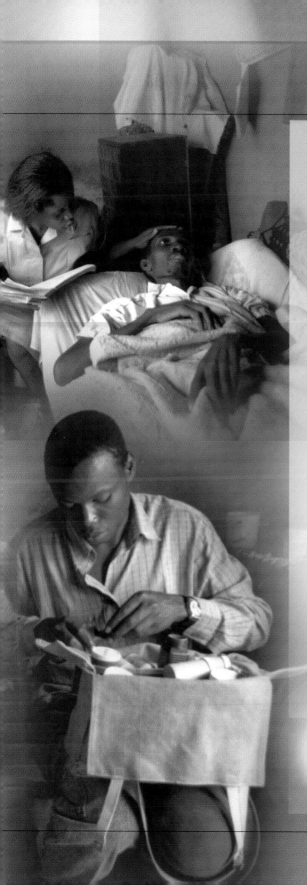

Out of Africa?

Some evidence suggests that the HIV and AIDS epidemic began in Africa, although it is hard to detect exactly how and why. A few people even argue that it was passed to humans from monkeys, which were killed and then eaten. The 1981–83 Central African cases of life-threatening Kaposi's sarcoma, meningitis and throat infections (which collectively became known as 'slim disease') seem to be related to the international **symptoms** of AIDS. The evidence goes back even further. HIV has been recovered from a blood sample taken from a patient who was tested in connection with a 1976 Ebola virus outbreak. Less conclusive evidence dates back to 1959 and beyond.

HIV did not become epidemic until the 1980s, perhaps because poor and young sexually active individuals **migrated** from rural areas to urban centres in developing countries. Their return to the countryside, coupled with international travel, tourism, and the international drug trade, helped spread the disease.

AIDS took hold in Africa in the 1980s, exhausting the limited medical resources of many countries.

Finding the root cause

By 1982 the term AIDS was widely known and the condition was being tracked across the world – as **fatalities** continued to rise. There was still agreement about its real cause, despite many competing theories. The link with male homosexuals seemed to be strong and research teams tried to link the condition with various practices engaged in by gay men, notably the use of certain drugs. Such studies reached dead-ends, especially as reports came in of concentrated occurrences of wasting diseases in Rwanda, Tanzania, Uganda, Zaire and Zambia – African nations with no real history of drug-taking. The African term for the final stages of this condition, 'slim disease', was an eerie echo of the **symptoms** being monitored in the USA and in other Western countries. There was still no real idea of the root cause, although in the course of 1982 the three modes of **transmission** were identified: sexual intercourse, mother-to-child and blood **transfusion**.

With this conclusion in mind, in 1983 the CDC warned **blood banks** of a possible problem with the blood supply. Later that year, scientists working at the *Institut Pasteur* (France) discovered and isolated the virus, which was then called the Human Immunodeficiency Virus (HIV). By now the medical world had a clear picture of the make-up of the HIV virus and the wider world could see its devastating effects. By 1985, at least one case of HIV or AIDS had been reported in each region of the world. At the same time, over 11,000 cases of AIDS had been **diagnosed** in the USA, including 5620 fatalities.

Giving blood is a safe activity despite misinformed scare stories that said it posed an HIV risk.

Dangerous misinformation

By the mid-1980s, the world was aware of the deadliness of HIV and AIDS but there was a great deal of ignorance about the causes of the condition and how it was spread. HIV-positive people were considered 'tainted' by many members of the public. This harmed efforts to increase public awareness of the disease. One family with three HIV-positive sons (**haemophiliacs** who had contracted the virus through blood transfusion) were driven from their home in Arcadia, Florida, after their house was burnt by people who thought that the boys would spread AIDS through the community.

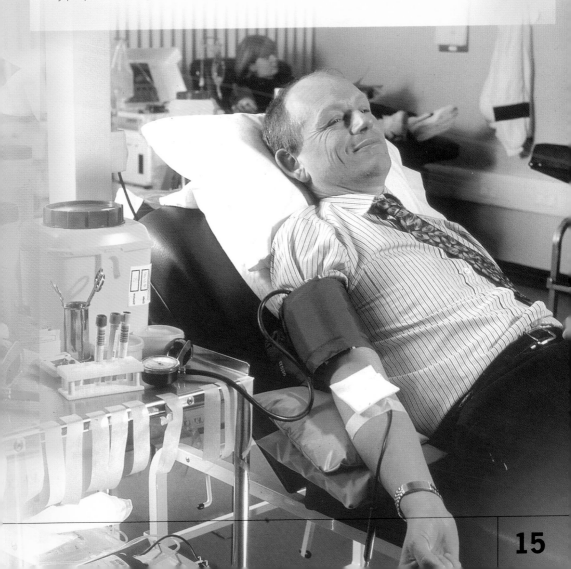

Recognizing the crisis

By the mid-1980s the medical community agreed on the main points surrounding HIV and AIDS: the virus at its heart, how it was transmitted and the sort of complications that it triggered as full blown AIDS set in. Many government and private organizations began to champion the causes of prevention, as well as research.

In 1984 four infants in Queensland, Australia, died from HIV-**contaminated** blood. A National AIDS Task Force was formed to advise the Australian Government on the scientific and medical aspects of the virus. Within a year Australia became the first country in the world to secure its blood supply from HIV infection by testing all donations. In 1986, the USA Food and Drug Administration (FDA) approved the first HIV **antibody** test, and HIV screening of blood donations began. At the same time, campaigning groups such as Act Up in the USA, and the Terrence Higgins Trust in the UK, set about publicizing the problem.

International efforts

Africa's first community-based response to AIDS was formed in Uganda in 1987. Called The AIDS Support Organization (TASO), it became a role model for similar activities around the world. That same year saw the founding of the Global Network of People living with HIV/AIDS and the World Health Organization (WHO) Special Programme on AIDS, later to become the Global Programme on AIDS. The International Council of AIDS Services Organizations (ICASO) was established in 1991.

Since that time, HIV and AIDS have remained in the headlines. New treatments are constantly being developed, and governments have recognized that this global crisis calls for a global response. The Joint United Nations Programme on HIV/AIDS (UNAIDS) was created in 1996 and has become the focal point of new research. In 2001, UN Secretary-General Kofi Annan launched his 'call to action', including the creation of a global fund on AIDS and health.

Focus on the problem spots

Sometimes outside groups are able to tackle aspects of the HIV and AIDS crisis where local governments have been hampered. One such group is the Futures Group Europe (FGE), based in Bath in the UK. The FGE bids for government funds to put in place projects aimed at education, prevention and counselling in an area defined as 'health management consultancy'. In the case of HIV and AIDS, 'health' refers to sexual health. It has been particularly successful in spreading essential information in some of the worst-affected parts of the world.

One of its projects concerns the high-risk provinces of Yunnan and Sichuan in China. Like many other governments of developing countries, Chinese officials were late to acknowledge the existence of the HIV infection within their borders. '"It can't happen here" is one of the sentiments that many government officials have,' says Jill Bausch, Managing Director of the Futures Group Europe. The Chinese project targets high-risk groups within Sichuan – **intravenous** drug users, commercial sex workers and their clients, men having sex with men and people already living with HIV or AIDS.

The FGE also helps manage government schemes to deal with the HIV and AIDS crisis in a more general manner. Some of this assistance, such as its work in Kenya, enables the country to channel money where it will be spent most usefully. Key areas include training medical personnel on promoting safe sex measures, distributing drugs to the most needy and developing services to support and assist people with AIDS.

Who gets HIV and AIDS?

Two important facts must be stressed in any discussion of who can **contract** HIV and AIDS. The first is that anyone can be at risk. Many people think 'it can't happen to me' because they think infection is limited solely to certain high-risk groups. The second fact is even simpler: in the twenty years of the current HIV and AIDS **epidemic**, no region or country has been spared.

Who's at risk?

AIDS researchers stress that although certain groups of people run a higher risk of contracting the HIV virus, it is their actions rather than their belonging to the group that puts them at risk. That risk derives from the ways in which we know that the HIV virus is **transmitted**. The virus is present in certain bodily fluids – blood, semen, vaginal fluids and breast milk. It is the transmission of any of these fluids from an infected person to someone else that passes on the risk of infection. In the broadest terms, the likeliest ways of transmitting these fluids are as follows:

- **vaginal sex** with an infected person
- **anal sex** with an infected person
- **oral sex** with an infected person
- sharing improperly cleaned **intravenous** needles with an infected person
- any exchange of blood, semen, vaginal fluids, or breast milk with an infected person.

Although once cruelly described as a 'gay plague', AIDS is a concern for anyone who has a sexual partner.

On safe ground

There are several important ways that you *cannot* get HIV. You cannot get it from:

- being bitten by insects or animals
- sharing most personal items with an HIV-infected person such as toilets, clothing or eating utensils
- touching a person with HIV or AIDS (this includes hugging and kissing)
- eating food with an HIV-infected person or eating food that has been prepared by an HIV-infected person
- going to public places which have been occupied by HIV-infected people
- being exposed to the sweat, saliva, or tears of an HIV-infected person
- giving blood, because a new, sterile needle is used for every donor.

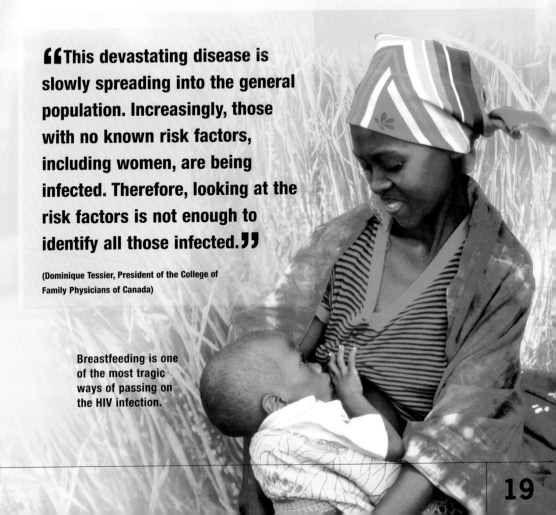

❝This devastating disease is slowly spreading into the general population. Increasingly, those with no known risk factors, including women, are being infected. Therefore, looking at the risk factors is not enough to identify all those infected.❞

(Dominique Tessier, President of the College of Family Physicians of Canada)

Breastfeeding is one of the most tragic ways of passing on the HIV infection.

19

Who gets HIV and AIDS?

In practical terms, this means people are at risk from HIV and AIDS if they have ever had unprotected sex (that is, sex without a condom) with any of the following: someone they know is infected with HIV or AIDS, someone who has ever injected drugs, someone who has shared needles with an infected person, or someone who has had sex with a person who shared needles. Having unprotected sex with multiple partners, or someone who's sexual history isn't known, puts a person at risk – as they cannot be sure that the partner is not infected. People are also at risk if they have ever used needles or syringes that have been used by someone else before they have used them.

This information bears out the conclusion that it is actions (or lack of them) that lead people into the high-risk category. Homosexual men need not be at higher risk, provided that they practice safe sex, including the use of condoms. Likewise, drug injectors – although they run many risks from the drugs themselves – can avoid the danger of contracting HIV by not sharing needles. In these cases it is the uninfected people who have the responsibility of reducing the risk to themselves. Unfortunately breast-feeding infants cannot make such a choice, so it is vital that mothers (and pregnant women) who are at risk have constant HIV tests. Even uninfected children born to HIV-infected mothers have an incidence of heart problems twelve times that of children in the general population.

USA breakdown

The Centers for Disease Control and Prevention (CDC) in Atlanta, Georgia, USA, is one of the most respected medical centres dealing with AIDS in the world. In addition to carrying out research into treatment and prevention, the CDC has compiled detailed records of all known HIV and AIDS cases within the USA. Its 2000 report breaks down overall figures along a number of lines. It uses the term 'method of exposure' to describe how individuals contracted the virus initially: men who have sex with men (47 per cent), injection drug users (25 per cent), heterosexual exposure (10 per cent) and blood or blood product infection (2 per cent). Males remain the more affected sex (82 per cent) although the female percentage has been rising throughout the **epidemic**. More worrying still, for women, is the fact that about two-thirds of people who contract HIV through heterosexual sex are women – largely because they are receiving bodily fluids (semen) from infected men.

CDC
CENTERS FOR DISEASE CONTROL AND PREVENTION

The CDC is the USA's leading disease research authority and has carried out extensive research into the treatment and prevention of HIV and AIDS. The protective suits and masks, used here to protect against the Ebola virus, are not necessary when dealing with HIV or AIDS.

Focus on Africa

Africa has been the hardest hit of all regions in the two decades since the AIDS **epidemic** became apparent around the world. The figures are staggering, and depressing, as they point to a whole generation that has been seriously affected by this deadly disease. Somewhere in the region of 80 per cent of all HIV infections (and AIDS deaths) occur in Africa, nearly all of them in the southern region known as sub-Saharan Africa.

The roots of the problem

There are many reasons for the widespread HIV infection in Africa. Many of them can be traced to the scattered, rural population within the region. Here, poor funding for education and health combines to keep people ignorant about HIV in the first place, and then unable to afford (or reach) medical treatment once they have become infected. Coupled with this funding issue is the social aspect: many traditional African societies frown on the types of safe-sex protection (particularly condoms) that have slowed the spread of HIV elsewhere. On top of this, come mixed signals from government leaders. For example, President Thabo Mbeki of South Africa, which has a serious HIV problem, has questioned the link between HIV and AIDS. Such views have worked against efforts to educate the population at large.

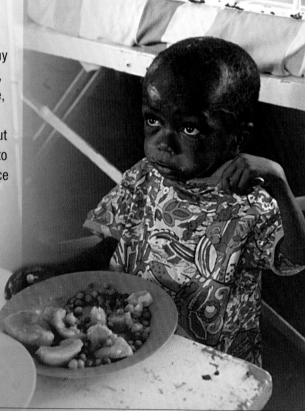

Many young children in Zaire – some of them HIV-positive themselves – have been left orphaned by the AIDS epidemic.

A way out?

There are, however, some glimmers of hope even in the worst-affected areas. Up to 35 per cent of Botswana's population is HIV-positive – making it the worst-hit country in the world. Life expectancy, once around 70 years, is now down to under 40. Recent efforts by the government, as well as the country's important diamond-mining companies, have led to widespread acceptance of safe sex methods. Debswana, the mining company that employs thousands of Botswana's men, funds HIV treatment for its employees and their wives. At the same time, the government has set in motion a programme to provide education, housing and health benefits for the many children who have been orphaned by AIDS. This combination of company and government might help turn the tide of infection in this once-prosperous nation. It could also, possibly, point to a solution for other countries.

Campaigners for an Aids Free Society (CAFS), on the streets of Nairobi, collect signatures for a petition to make HIV/AIDS medicines more affordable and accessible to Kenyans living with the disease.

The virus at work

The progression from the initial HIV infection to the clinical diseases that define AIDS may take six to ten years or more. During this time the HIV virus works – and eventually leads to AIDS itself – by attacking the body's **immune system** and making it much less capable of fighting off disease. It kills **T-cells** within the white blood cells, which are the major disease fighters in the body. It invades the cells and actually manages to replace their **DNA** so that the cells no longer produce new T-cells, but produce new HIV viruses instead.

The hidden infection

HIV is often **symptom**-free, but within one to three weeks after infection some people experience flu-like symptoms such as fever, headache, skin rash, tender **lymph nodes** and a sense of discomfort. These symptoms last about one to two weeks. During this phase, HIV reproduces to very high concentrations in the blood, **mutates** (changes its make-up) frequently and establishes infections throughout the body. The infected person's T-cell count falls briefly but then returns to near normal levels as the immune system responds to the infection. Individuals are thought to be highly infectious during this phase. The next phase of the infection is the longest and can last for periods of ten years or more. HIV-positive people exhibit few symptoms of disease and T-cell counts – an important measure in testing and treating the condition – range from low to normal (500 to 1000 cells per cubic millimetre of blood). However, the HIV continues to spread during this phase, destroying the immune system.

Tests can determine whether swollen lymph nodes are an early symptom of HIV infection or simply an indication of a cold or flu.

24

The final phases

Eventually, the infected person enters the final phases of the infection when their symptoms become obvious. T-cell counts fall (down to 200 cells per cubic millimetre of blood) and the first of the **opportunistic infections** set in, although at first these are not life-threatening. Up to a year may pass before fully blown AIDS develops. T-cell counts stay below 200 (a figure that many doctors use as a signal of AIDS) and the person loses weight and energy. Death caused by severe life-threatening opportunistic infections and cancers occurs within one to two years.

This patient has marks on his face and neck caused by the cancer 'Kaposi's sarcoma' – a common symptom of AIDS.

Family and friends

It is always a terrible shock when someone finds out that they are HIV-positive. Rightly or wrongly, many people interpret a positive test result as a 'death sentence', even though there is an increasing range of treatments to slow the progress of the HIV virus – perhaps buying vital time until there is more medical progress. These initial fears and anxieties are often made worse when the HIV-positive individual tells their friends and family about their condition.

Rejection and denial

Telling the family about an HIV infection is often the first time that the infected person has told that they are gay, or possibly an **intravenous** drug user. 'Coming out' in these circumstances is a painful experience. The double effect of learning that, for example, a son or brother is both gay and HIV-positive can tear some families apart. 'It can't happen to us' is the reaction sometimes, as some family members go into a state of **denial** about their loved one's condition – just when he or she needs help most. Of course, this is not always the family's reaction and many of the most committed AIDS activists are those with a family member who is HIV-positive.

The same risk of denial can happen to friends, although many HIV-positive people trust in the old saying that 'you can choose your friends but not your family'. In a sense, they hope that their friends will understand what they are going through. However, even close friends can be badly informed about how HIV and AIDS is **transmitted**. Such people might shy away from an HIV-positive individual, so that it is only the 'true friends' who remain to provide support and reassurance. The peeling away of seemingly strong friendships can cause great distress for infected people.

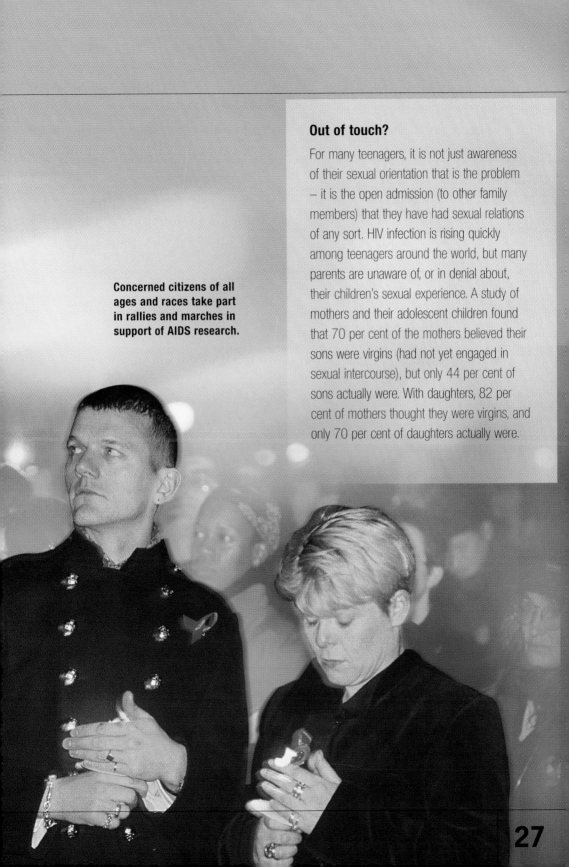

Concerned citizens of all ages and races take part in rallies and marches in support of AIDS research.

Out of touch?

For many teenagers, it is not just awareness of their sexual orientation that is the problem – it is the open admission (to other family members) that they have had sexual relations of any sort. HIV infection is rising quickly among teenagers around the world, but many parents are unaware of, or in denial about, their children's sexual experience. A study of mothers and their adolescent children found that 70 per cent of the mothers believed their sons were virgins (had not yet engaged in sexual intercourse), but only 44 per cent of sons actually were. With daughters, 82 per cent of mothers thought they were virgins, and only 70 per cent of daughters actually were.

Taking precautions

Because there is as yet no successful vaccination against HIV, prevention efforts have focused mainly on educating the public about how HIV is passed on and about personal measures that reduce the risk of infection.

The USA's AIDS activist group Act Up, which was formed in the mid-1980s just as the scope of the problem was becoming clear, was one of the first organizations to grasp the fact that ignorance and carelessness were the two biggest obstacles in combating the spread of AIDS. With a series of eye-catching posters and other images, the group pressed home the message in **unequivocal** terms: 'Silence is Death'. Other groups at local, national and international levels have echoed this message.

Public efforts

In the USA, the Centers for Disease Control and Prevention has established the National AIDS Clearinghouse, a telephone hotline that enables callers to obtain educational literature and current statistics on AIDS. On a wider level, safe-sex campaigns encourage sexual **abstinence** (avoiding sexual contact) or **monogamy** (having only one sexual partner) as ways of slowing the spread. They also urge people to use condoms in order to provide a protective barrier during sexual intercourse.

Of course, sexual activity is only one way of **transmitting** HIV. Many governments have taken action to deal with the spread of the infection among **intravenous** (IV) drug users. They have also set up programmes to check all blood used for **transfusions**. Needle-exchange programmes reduce needle sharing and consequent HIV transmission among IV drug abusers. The same risk, however, holds for medical personnel who must handle infected equipment on a daily basis. Again, governments have set strict guidelines for the use of protective clothing and proper instrument disposal.

Artist, Keith Haring died of AIDS in 1990. Before his death he created works of art to raise awareness of the disease, and the importance of safe sex.

The safe sex message

The most important precaution against HIV infection for most people is safe sex, and it is this message that HIV and AIDS awareness groups around the world are preaching. Safe sex means sex that is absolutely safe, compared with many activities that could possibly spread the HIV infection.

The first rule is to use a condom during sexual intercourse. Using a condom, however, is not absolutely safe as condoms can break. The bigger problem for safe-sex campaigners is the unwillingness of some people to use condoms even when they know that it is the safe way to behave. There are many reasons for this unwillingness. Some people fear that a new partner will think that they have 'something to hide' if they suggest using a condom. The message for these people, however, remains just as firm: one careless act could lead to the infection.

Oral sex (one person kissing, licking or sucking the sexual areas of another person) does carry some risk of infection. However, infection from oral sex alone seems to be very rare.

Absolutely safe sex

The safest sex, of course, is no sex at all. 'No sex' really means no sexual contact where fluids (which could pass on infection) are exchanged. Most countries have laws making it illegal for young teenagers to have full sexual relations. The dangers of passing on or receiving the HIV infection show that these laws make sense.

However, lots of activities are completely safe. These include kissing, cuddling, and massaging and rubbing each other's bodies. Remember though, if you have any cuts or sores on your hands make sure they are covered with plasters.

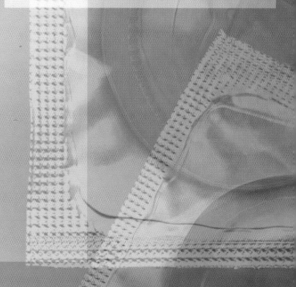

❝I carry condoms – I get them from the clinic and I'm on the pill as well to protect me from pregnancy… but I'd still want him to wear a condom.❞

(Teenager quoted in Avert's HIV & AIDS booklet)

Condoms play a central role in the safe-sex campaign.

The medical response

The body of medical knowledge about HIV and AIDS, built over two decades of research and observation, has led to a number of treatments. It has also provided a few clues about which paths to follow in future research. Most of it has been based on the idea that it is the initial HIV infection that triggers the long-term destruction of the **immune system**, leading eventually to the condition known as AIDS. A few medical voices have challenged this assumption (see panel on page 35), arguing that the link between HIV and AIDS is less clear-cut. However, the treatments developed so far have all dealt with the HIV infection and ways to slow it down.

The medicines available

The main HIV treatments are **antiviral** drugs, which try to stop the HIV virus from making copies of itself. Specifically, they aim to block a stage in the virus's life called 'reverse transcription'. HIV can only become infectious after an **enzyme** known as reverse transcriptase (RT) performs this job. Many HIV drugs, including AZT (zidovudine), work as RT **inhibitors**. Although drugs such as AZT were never considered a cure for HIV infection, doctors believe that they slow the progress of AIDS. AZT also reduces HIV **transmission** from pregnant women to their babies.

AIDS RESEARCH LABORATORY

AUTHORIZED PERSONNEL ONLY
1. GOWNS MUST BE WORN
2. GLOVES MUST BE USED
3. WASH HANDS

CAUTION

EXPERIMENT
IN PROGRESS

AZT, an RT inhibitor, is one of the most highly publicized medical treatments to stem the progress of AIDS.

Because HIV **mutates** frequently during the earliest period of infection, an HIV-infected person carries many different types of HIV. Some of these types may be able to survive drugs used against them. By **diagnosing** HIV infection early on (before very many variations of the virus have developed), doctors have a better chance of succeeding with treatment.

A more recent class of anti-HIV drugs, developed in the mid-1990s, are known as 'protease inhibitors'. They work by crippling a key enzyme called protease, which is vital to HIV in later stages of infection. When the HIV protease enzyme is blocked, the virus cannot reproduce. When protease inhibitors are taken in combination with other anti-HIV drugs; they have been shown to reduce levels of the virus, sometimes dramatically, to raise the **T-cell** count (an indicator of the immune system) and to reduce **mortality** rates.

The medical response

Later infections

A number of drugs combat the many AIDS-associated **opportunistic infections**. These treatments have provided clinical benefit and prolonged survival for individuals with AIDS. **Antifungal** drugs are effective against AIDS-related **fungal infections**. Certain drugs used to treat herpes infection also help to treat CMV retinitis (a disease that affects sight) and other AIDS-related herpes diseases.

The way ahead

Gene therapy, a technique that involves altering the genes of the infected person to help prevent the virus from spreading to uninfected cells, might someday be used to treat HIV infection. Gene therapy has been used in experimental trials to **inhibit** HIV. Gene therapy has also been used to introduce a new gene that protects the cells from becoming infected by HIV.

In addition, governments and medical researchers are looking for ways to develop an effective **immunization** programme. Such a widespread series of medical injections could be either protective (preventing infection if an immunized person is exposed to HIV) or **therapeutic**, prolonging survival or decreasing immune destruction in people already infected with HIV. The World Health Organization (WHO) is currently funding large-scale trials of protective vaccines in areas of the world where the rate of HIV infection is rising quickly.

> **❝AIDS is no longer associated with a death sentence immediately. People feel it's less serious ... because there are drugs that can help them. What they don't realize is these drugs are not a cure.❞**
>
> **(Dr Donald Gelhorn, president of the College of Family Physicians of Canada)**

Dissenting voices

The huge cost of AIDS research in the two decades since the **epidemic** was first identified, coupled with the lack of any real sign of a cure, has caused some scientists to think of new ways of approaching the problem. Many scientists believe that the HIV virus is not the culprit in this epidemic. Either because it is too simple to produce such wide-ranging effects or that it is just one of many 'triggers' that bring on the AIDS condition. Some even argue that the high-powered drugs used for treatment – especially AZT – are actually part of the problem. Rather than boosting the body's natural **immune system**, they argue, such drugs are actually weakening it and hastening – rather than delaying – the onset of AIDS.

Bill Gates, Head of Microsoft, announced a $100 million boost for AIDS research in June 2001.

Counting the cost

More than 90 per cent of all HIV infections worldwide have occurred in developing countries. The tragedy is that for most people in those countries, the new HIV treatments, which can cost up to $15,000 a year for each individual, are much too expensive. Many developing countries with high rates of HIV infection cannot afford the most basic medical treatments, much less these expensive new treatments. The majority of people infected with HIV in the USA and other developed countries are also poor and many are drug users who might have difficulty gaining access to the latest treatments.

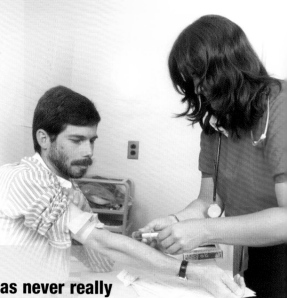

❝I think zidovudine [AZT] was never really evaluated properly and that its efficacy has never been proved, but its toxicity certainly is important. And I think it has killed a lot of people. Especially at the high doses. I personally think it not worth using alone or in combination at all.❞

(Dr Andrew Herxheimer, Emeritus Professor of Pharmacology, Cochrane Centre, Oxford, quoted in *Continuum* October 2000)

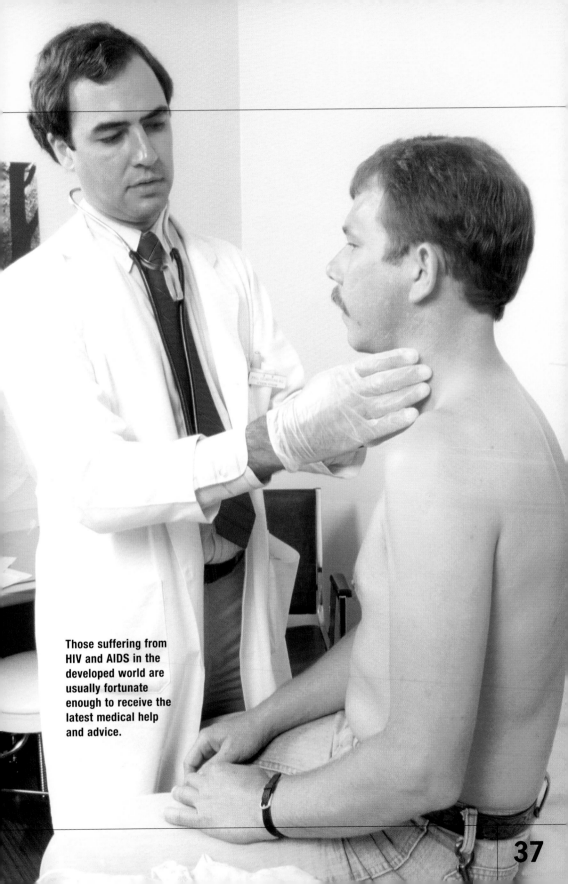

Those suffering from HIV and AIDS in the developed world are usually fortunate enough to receive the latest medical help and advice.

Public health

Public health, the term used to describe medical-awareness campaigns at a national or international level, plays an important part in the fight against HIV and AIDS. Specific campaigns – aimed at gay men in Toronto, prostitutes in Uganda, drug users in Glasgow – stress the importance of sensible behaviour among known high-risk groups. Many of these efforts are co-ordinated by government or international organizations such as the World Health Organization.

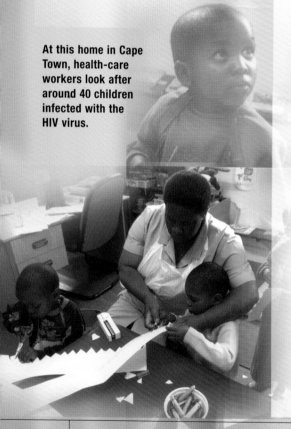

At this home in Cape Town, health-care workers look after around 40 children infected with the HIV virus.

A social issue

Many people consider that HIV infection and AIDS can be completely prevented, if not cured, because the methods of HIV **transmission** are so well known. It is this belief that lies behind safe-sex campaigns, (especially arguments for wider distribution of condoms) as well as programmes for needle exchange among **intravenous** drug users.
Such campaigns, however, often meet with disapproval from many elements in society. These people believe that prevention efforts that involve frank discussion of sexuality and condom distribution in schools encourages sexual activity. They also argue that needle-exchange programmes promote drug abuse.

The wrong direction?

The lack of effective vaccines and **antiviral** drugs for AIDS has led some people to suggest that there is not enough funding for AIDS research. This accusation crops up frequently in the USA, where there are the **facilities** – and the national wealth – to make a difference. Although the actual amount of government funding for AIDS research is large, most of the money is used for expensive clinical studies to test new drugs. Some scientists argue that not enough is known about the basic biological structure of HIV. They recommend shifting the emphasis of AIDS research to basic research that could ultimately result in more effective medicines.

There is another viewpoint, however, about the whole issue of government funding of HIV and AIDS research. In most developed countries, such as the USA, UK and Australia, this funding nearly matches that of heart and cancer research, 2 diseases that kill 15 to 25 times as many people as AIDS. There is no easy answer.

"We're concerned about these individuals ... because we know that early treatment can help extend their life and ensure that they do not infect others, including their newborn children."

(Dr Donald Gelhorn, president of the College of Family Physicians of Canada)

Legal matters

In addition to the day-to-day problems of looking after their health and maintaining an upbeat attitude, HIV-positive individuals and AIDS patients have a wide range of legal matters to address. Some of these relate to reaffirming their rights as citizens in the face of **discrimination** and ignorance about HIV. Then there are other, more personal, matters to deal with on an individual basis: some of these need the assistance of trained legal personnel.

Government measures

The USA's government has been a leader in trying to assist HIV-infected individuals, both through legislation and through additional community-funding measures. In 1990 HIV-infected people were included in the Americans with Disabilities Act, making discrimination against people with AIDS for jobs, housing and other social benefits illegal. Another legal measure, the Ryan White Comprehensive AIDS Resources Emergency Act, established a community-funding programme designed to assist in the daily lives of people living with AIDS. This congressional act was named in memory of a young man who contracted HIV through blood products and became a public figure for his courage in fighting the disease and community prejudice. Ryan White, a **haemophiliac** who was infected with HIV through **contaminated** blood products, had faced discrimination and was blocked from attending school. He died of AIDS at the age of eighteen. The act is still in place, although continued funding for such social programs is under debate by current legislators.

The tragic story of Ryan White helped increase public awareness of HIV and AIDS in the USA.

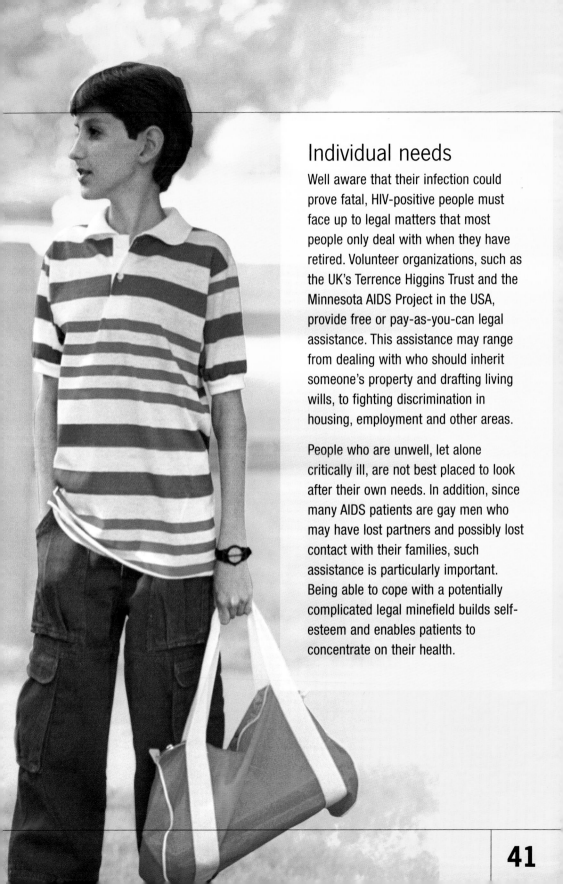

Individual needs

Well aware that their infection could prove fatal, HIV-positive people must face up to legal matters that most people only deal with when they have retired. Volunteer organizations, such as the UK's Terrence Higgins Trust and the Minnesota AIDS Project in the USA, provide free or pay-as-you-can legal assistance. This assistance may range from dealing with who should inherit someone's property and drafting living wills, to fighting discrimination in housing, employment and other areas.

People who are unwell, let alone critically ill, are not best placed to look after their own needs. In addition, since many AIDS patients are gay men who may have lost partners and possibly lost contact with their families, such assistance is particularly important. Being able to cope with a potentially complicated legal minefield builds self-esteem and enables patients to concentrate on their health.

Life with HIV and AIDS

News of a positive result from an HIV test can be extremely unsettling for anyone. It means having to adjust nearly every aspect of life – job expectations, friendships, family commitments and many other features – in the face of what is likely to be a long and hard journey. Yet there are many ways in which HIV-positive individuals and people with AIDS can manage to live a normal, or nearly normal, life. In fact, the chances of continued health often depend on their being able to cope with the stress of HIV infection calmly and with support. Sometimes the sense of isolation is one of the hardest feelings to address. This is why volunteer groups mean so much to those with either HIV or AIDS.

Outside help

The Minnesota AIDS Project is typical of the many local and regional groups that help HIV-positive individuals and people with AIDS to live as normal a life as possible. This help can take the form of face-to-face meetings with social workers who can advise on practical matters such as government paper work, insurance and legal matters (see previous pages). Like similar organizations, the Minnesota AIDS Project uses a phone hotline to keep communication easy, even when the patient is on his or her own.

It sometimes takes an outsider to remind an HIV-positive person that they need to relax and enjoy themselves as much as possible if they are to cope with the stresses and strains that are certain to develop. This advice often comes from a 'buddy' – a volunteer who specializes in giving care and providing community for HIV-positive people throughout their illness. The 'buddy' system originated in San Francisco and New York, cities with an early and high incidence of HIV. The semi-formal arrangement at the outset usually

develops into a more caring relationship. Many people, particularly those who have AIDS, have found that their 'buddies' have become a lifeline and an essential source of comfort. 'Home helpers' – also usually volunteers – help with household chores such as cleaning, cooking and shopping.

The Minnesota AIDS Project, like other HIV and AIDS civic groups, provides a lifeline for those too ill, isolated or afraid to meet others.

The wider picture

Public figures and celebrities who are themselves HIV infected or who have died from AIDS – including the basketball player Magic Johnson, the actor Rock Hudson, the singer Freddy Mercury and tennis player Arthur Ashe – have given rise to a wider public understanding of AIDS. This has helped society at large come to grips with the **epidemic**. It might seem odd, but these sometimes tragic case histories have actually improved the quality of life for other HIV and AIDS individuals who now encounter more sympathy from those they meet every day.

The AIDS quilt

As a tribute to people who have died from AIDS, friends and families of American AIDS victims stitched together a giant quilt in which each panel of the quilt was dedicated to the memory of someone who had died from AIDS. For more than a decade, this quilt has travelled from community to community in the USA to promote AIDS awareness. Although it provides no obvious help for those currently with HIV or AIDS, it emphasizes the sense of loss from the wider community, generating more understanding of the disease, as well as more donations for future research.

The AIDS quilt literally links the stories of hundreds of Americans who have died over the course of more than twenty years.

Arthur Ashe, the American tennis great, was one of the first high profile victims of AIDS.

Dealing with the treatment

Sometimes the treatment for HIV seems in itself to cause illness and discomfort. Those HIV-positive people who take 'drug cocktails' (protease **inhibitors**, taken in combination with other **antiviral** drugs such as AZT) often experience serious side effects, rather like those of cancer patients who are undergoing **chemotherapy**. These combination treatments are highly **toxic**, and act like a poison in the body by causing vomiting and cramps. Many people cannot withstand these effects, and have to stop taking the treatments. Moreover, it is difficult to keep to such a treatment because it involves taking an enormous number of pills (on average twenty per day) at strict intervals and under specific conditions. For example, some drugs must be taken on an empty stomach in the middle of the day, others on a full stomach at night – some need to be taken with fatty foods, and some with liquids. Already plagued by stress (combined drug therapies cost $15,000 to $20,000 per year for medication alone), many people simply cannot cope with the requirements.

Treatment and counselling

HIV and AIDS can only be treated when potential patients are aware of the risk of infection and choose to deal with that risk. So, in a sense, 'treatment' for people who have been exposed to a risk refers to a readiness to have regular HIV tests, even after the first one or two have shown negative results. A positive result, with all its implications for the patient, calls for treatment of a more medical nature (see pages 32–37) as well as counselling to help deal with the stresses of living with the HIV infection.

Some people even benefit from counselling if they have had a negative result. They must come to terms with the fact that they might have been exposed to a deadly infection, and that the next test might prove to be positive.

Testing

AIDS cannot be **diagnosed** with a single test. However, HIV can be found by one of several blood tests. The ELISA is the most common HIV test. It is a blood test that checks to see if there are any HIV **antibodies** in the blood. In other words, it doesn't check for the virus itself – it checks to see whether the body is trying

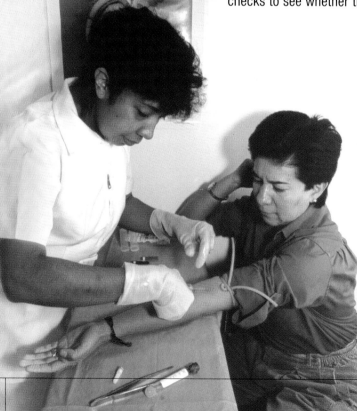

Frequent tests are the best way of monitoring HIV, both in an individual and in the community at large.

to fight the virus. Another common type of test is the Western blot, which is used to confirm the results of an ELISA. The Indirect Immunofluorescence Assay (IFA) is another test used in the same way as the Western blot.

Both the Western blot and the IFA are blood tests. An ELISA (HIV test), confirmed by a Western blot or IFA, is considered virtually 100 per cent accurate, although other factors can affect accuracy. There are other tests available, but they are used mostly for laboratory research, and some are expensive and complicated.

The Centers for Disease Control and Prevention recommends waiting three to six months after exposure to HIV before testing. This is because the ELISA is an antibody test, and it is important to give the antibodies enough time to develop in the blood and be found. If a person tests too early, there may not be enough antibodies to show up on the test yet, and they could get a false negative result when they really do have HIV.

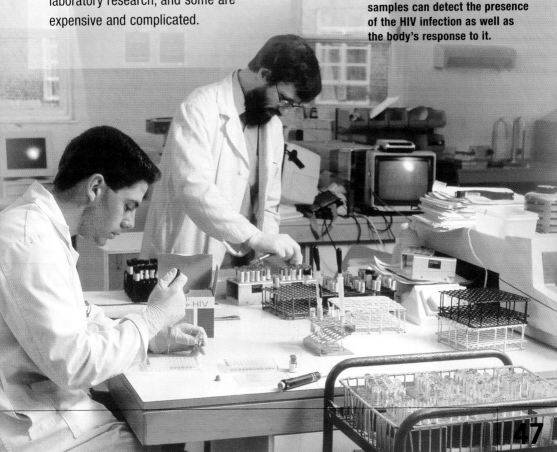

Detailed studies of blood samples can detect the presence of the HIV infection as well as the body's response to it.

Counselling

Even if it has been hard to develop medical treatments to deal with HIV and AIDS, the broader issues have been somewhat easier to address. Counselling plays an important part in helping people come to terms with what is probably going to become a life-threatening condition. However, just as no two people react to difficult news in the same way, counselling must also come in 'all shapes and sizes'.

Most people find that the best part of counselling is being able to talk, as well as to listen. Those with AIDS or HIV infection are usually well informed about what the infection is, how they might have got it and what sort of medical treatments are available. Counselling provides them with something else – a way of expressing their own feelings. This might take place in a one-to-one setting, speaking to a professional counsellor or to a 'buddy' (a volunteer working for an AIDS charity). Or it might work better in a group, where individuals have a chance to describe their own experiences and to benefit from hearing other people's stories.

Fears often become less alarming when people realize that others are facing the same problems and they are not alone. AIDS charities have set up extensive networks for those people infected with HIV. They list individual counselling centres as well as groups. Most medical centres also have similar information, and doctors, nurses and other medical professionals can advise people on the nearest testing centres as well as counselling opportunities.

Test counselling

Many testing centres provide both pre- and post-test counselling. Counsellors will talk about past behaviour, future behaviour, test anxiety, fear of death and many other matters relating to HIV and AIDS. People who are at all nervous about the test often find that it is a good idea to talk to a counsellor. There may be independent counselling or support groups in your area, and these are best contacted through one of the organizations listed on pages 52 and 53.

AIDS test counselling sessions can take some of the acute worry out of a process that many people avoid out of fear.

People to talk to

'Ignorance is death' read the posters first produced by the AIDS awareness charity Act Up in the 1980s. By the same token, knowledge can preserve or prolong life in the face of the deadly HIV infection. That knowledge, for most young people, comes from frank discussions with teachers, volunteers, medical personnel but most importantly, with their own parents.

Breaking the ice

Unfortunately, most parents do not find it easy to deal with the issue of HIV and AIDS, at least in relation to their own children. Perhaps it is the scope of the disease that puts them off, or the idea that it is too soon to be discussing sex and sexuality. A survey in the USA of pre-adolescents and their parents in a high-risk HIV neighbourhood found that parents overestimate how much they talk about HIV. Kids remembered less than one-fourth of HIV discussions parents said had occurred. They were most likely to remember talks with their parents that were private.

Parents can influence their children's actions and children recognize this fact – even if the parents themselves do not realize it. For a sensible conversation to take place, both parents and children must often shed their preconceptions – parents losing their fear of being too 'liberal', and children of being criticized. The younger generation faces a deadly future unless lines of communication remain open.

The classroom is an ideal setting to learn about HIV and AIDS.

Other voices

Luckily, young people do not need to rely on just their families to talk about HIV and AIDS. Most family doctors can advise young people on the disease itself and also on how to find more information and people to explain more about HIV and AIDS. Many AIDS charities, such as the UK's Terrence Higgins Trust, talk to young people through links developed with medical centres and with schools. This Trust, as well as other groups listed on pages 52 and 53, provide excellent starting points if young people need to find experienced (and sympathetic) people who can listen to their concerns.

❝I think it's sad I can't talk to my mom about it – but it's her loss. I can always go other places. I think that is a lot of the problem, because when you go to 'other places' sometimes you get the wrong information.❞

(Teenager, quoted by the Center for AIDS Prevention Studies on the University of California San Francisco web site)

Charities such as the UK's Terrence Higgins Trust provide informed advice on HIV and AIDS while raising money for further research.

51

Information and advice

The following organizations have a special interest in providing information and advice about HIV infection and AIDS. They are grouped below in several sections: international as well as regional areas that can provide exact advice for specific locations within a country. Many of these organizations operate almost exclusively over the Internet, so web site addresses are listed in addition to (where relevant) telephone numbers and postal addresses.

International Contacts

ÆGIS, www.aegis.com
Pronounced 'EE-jis', this organization connects over 32,000 electronic bulletin boards in 66 countries to provide information and to relieve some of the suffering and isolation caused by HIV and AIDS.

The joint United Nations Programme on HIV/AIDS (UNAIDS), www.unaids.org
The United Nations brought six organizations together in a joint and co-sponsored programme in 1996.

AIDS.ORG, www.immunet.org
Since 1995, Immunet has produced the essential AIDS.ORG web site, and has been a pioneer in the global online distribution of quality HIV and AIDS information as well as providing the non-profit Immunet AIDS Bookstore.

Contacts in the UK

AVERT, www.avert.org
4 Brighton Road, Horsham, West Sussex, RH13 5BA
Tel: 01403 210202 Fax: 01403 211001
AVERT is a national AIDS charity which aims to use education to prevent people from becoming infected with HIV.

Terrence Higgins Trust
Tel: 020 7242 1010 (helpline)
e-mail: info@tht.org.uk
The Terrence Higgins Trust is the leading HIV and AIDS charity in the UK.

Contacts in the USA

Advocates for Youth
www.advocatesforyouth.org
Suite 200, 1025 Vermont Avenue NW
Washington, DC 20005
Tel: 202/347-5700
Advocates for Youth tackles problems relating to a wide range of young people's concerns, and its information on HIV and AIDS is up-to-date and informative.

American Red Cross, www.redcross.org
AIDS Education Office, 8111 Gate-house Road Falls Church, VA 22042
The Red Cross is experienced in dealing with passing on clear and detailed information about all aspects of health; this office concentrates on its vast fund of knowledge about HIV and AIDS.

The Centers for Disease Control and Prevention (CDC), www.cdc.gov
Located in Atlanta, Georgia, CDC is an agency of the Department of Health and Human Services. Its aim is to promote health and quality of life by preventing and controlling disease, injury, and disability.

CDC National Prevention Information Network
www.cdcnpin.org
Tel: 1-800-458-523
e-mail: info@cdcnpin.org
This organization has a large amount of information on all aspects of HIV and AIDS.

National AIDS Hotline
Tel: 1-800-342-AIDS
National Teen AIDS Hotline
Tel: 1-800-440-TEEN
The National AIDS Hotline can be contacted 24 hours-a-day. They are extremely helpful, and have all the latest Red Cross information, a wide range of information pamphlets and a large computer database of HIV testing sites throughout the USA. The National Teen AIDS Hotline operates every Friday and Saturday evening from 6pm until midnight, Eastern Time.

Contacts in Canada
The Community AIDS Treatment Information Exchange (CATIE)
www.catie.ca
This independent, non-profit community-based organization offers services across Canada through the HIV/AIDS Treatment Information Network.

Contacts in Australia and New Zealand

The ABC's AIDS: Where are we now?
www.abc.net.au/science/slab/aids
Produced by the Australian Broadcasting Corporation, this web site provides essential information about prevention and progress within the whole HIV topic.

AIDSLINE, www.vicnet.net.au/vicnet /community/aidsline.html
Tel: 039347 6099
toll-free: 1800 133 392
AIDSLINE is Victoria's telephone counselling, information and referral service on HIV, AIDS and all other sexually transmitted diseases.

The Bobby Goldsmith Foundation (BGF)
www.bgf.org.au
The Bobby Goldsmith Foundation's mission is to assist people directly disadvantaged by HIV and

AIDS in NSW, to maintain a reasonable quality of life through the provision of financial assistance, financial counselling and supported housing.

The National AIDS Treatment Advocacy Project (NATAP), www.natap.org
NATPA strives to provide the very latest in HIV drug development, research and treatment information. The most current research directions and antiretroviral drug data is provided on this web site.

Further Reading
AIDS
by Jo Whelan. Hodder Wayland, 2001

AIDS: Why Should I Care?
by Robert Starr. People Taking Action Against AIDS, 1999

EveryBody: preventing HIV and other Sexually Transmitted Diseases, revised edition
by Deborah Schoeberlein. RAD Educational Programs, April 2001.

Risky Times: How to Be AIDS-Smart and Stay Healthy/Book With Parent's Guide
by Jeanne Blake and Beth Winship. Workman Publishing, 1990

Teen Guide to Safe Sex
by Alan E. Nourse. Franklin Watts, February 1989

Teen Sex: risks and consequences (Perspectives on Healthy Sexuality)
by Julie K. Endersbe. Capstone Press, September 1999

Disclaimer
All the Internet addresses (URLs) given in this book were valid at the time of going to press. However, due to the dynamic nature of the Internet, some addresses may have changed, or sites may have ceased to exist since publication. While the author and publishers regret any inconvenience this may cause readers, no responsibility for any such changes can be accepted by either the author or the publishers.

Glossary

abrasion
small cut or opening on the surface of the skin

abstinence
choosing not to do something (for example have sexual relations)

anal sex
sexual contact between a penis and someone else's anus

antibody
protein produced by cells in the lymph system to fight 'invaders' within the body

antifungal
designed to combat or work against a fungal infection

antiviral
designed to combat or work against a virus

blood bank
place where blood that has been donated by volunteers is stored, to be used for medical operations

chemotherapy
course of high-powered drugs (chemicals) that many cancer patients take to combat the cancerous growth

contaminated
carrying an infection

contract
to pick up or catch (as a disease)

denial
(in human behaviour) an unwillingness to accept or deal with an unpleasant truth

diagnose
to make a clear-cut medical decision about the cause of a condition

discrimination
denying individuals (or groups) normal human or legal rights because of their race, religion, sexual orientation etc.

DNA
Deoxyribonucleic Acid, the essential 'storehouse' of a living organism's genetic information and present in every cell

efficacy
ability to do a job

enzyme
protein present in cells which enables chemical changes to take place

epidemic
disease affecting many people at the same time

facilities
full range of equipment available to do a job

fatalities
deaths as a result of a disease

fungal infection
infection caused by an organism known as a fungus, ranging from mild infections such as athlete's foot to possibly deadly infections of the lungs

haemophiliac
person suffering from a disease that affects the cells in the blood that help form clots when someone has a cut

immune system
overall network of natural defences that the body uses to combat infection

immunization
wide-ranging effort to provide drugs or other medicines to help people become immune to (unable to be infected by) a certain disease

inhibitor
something that slows or stops the ability of another substance to work

intravenous
(usually referring to drugs) taken by a needle that is inserted into a vein

Kaposi's sarcoma
type of cancer that causes blotches to appear on the skin

lymph nodes (glands)
part of the body that helps prevent the spread of infection

migration
movement of many people in the same direction at the same time

monogamy
sexual relations with only one partner

mortality
(medically) referring to levels of death caused by a certain disease or condition

mutate
to change the form of the genes inside a cell by an accident

opportunistic infection
normally harmless virus that becomes dangerous in persons with a damaged immune system

oral sex
sexual contact between someone's mouth and someone else's vagina or penis

pneumonia
infectious disease that causes fluid to form and collect in the lungs

secretion
naturally produced fluid inside the body

symptom
sign (usually outward) of an underlying disease or condition

syndrome
set of symptoms which occur together

T-cell
essential conductors of the immune system, which turn on antibody production

therapeutic
aimed at relieving some of the symptoms of a disease

toxic
poisonous to the human body

toxicity
how toxic something is

transfusion
transfer of blood to someone who needs it for medical reasons

transmit
to pass on a disease to someone else

tuberculosis
illness of the lungs that weakens a person and can lead to death

unequivocal
with absolute certainty

vaginal sex
sex involving a penis being inserted into a vagina

Index

Titles in the *Need to Know* series include:

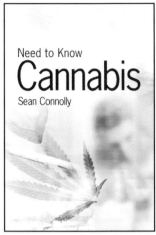

Need to Know
Cannabis
Sean Connolly

Hardback   0 431 09795 X

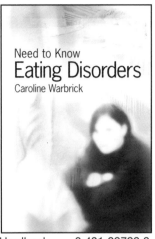

Need to Know
Eating Disorders
Caroline Warbrick

Hardback   0 431 09799 2

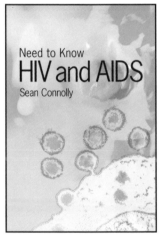

Need to Know
HIV and AIDS
Sean Connolly

Hardback   0 431 09796 8

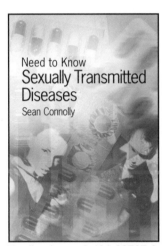

Need to Know
Sexually Transmitted Diseases
Sean Connolly

Hardback   0 431 09797 6

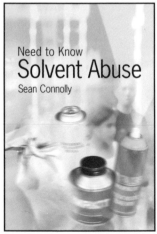

Need to Know
Solvent Abuse
Sean Connolly

Hardback   0 431 09794 1

Need to Know
Teenage Pregnancy
Mary Nolan

Hardback   0 431 09798 4

Find out about the other titles in this series on our website www.heinemann.co.uk/library